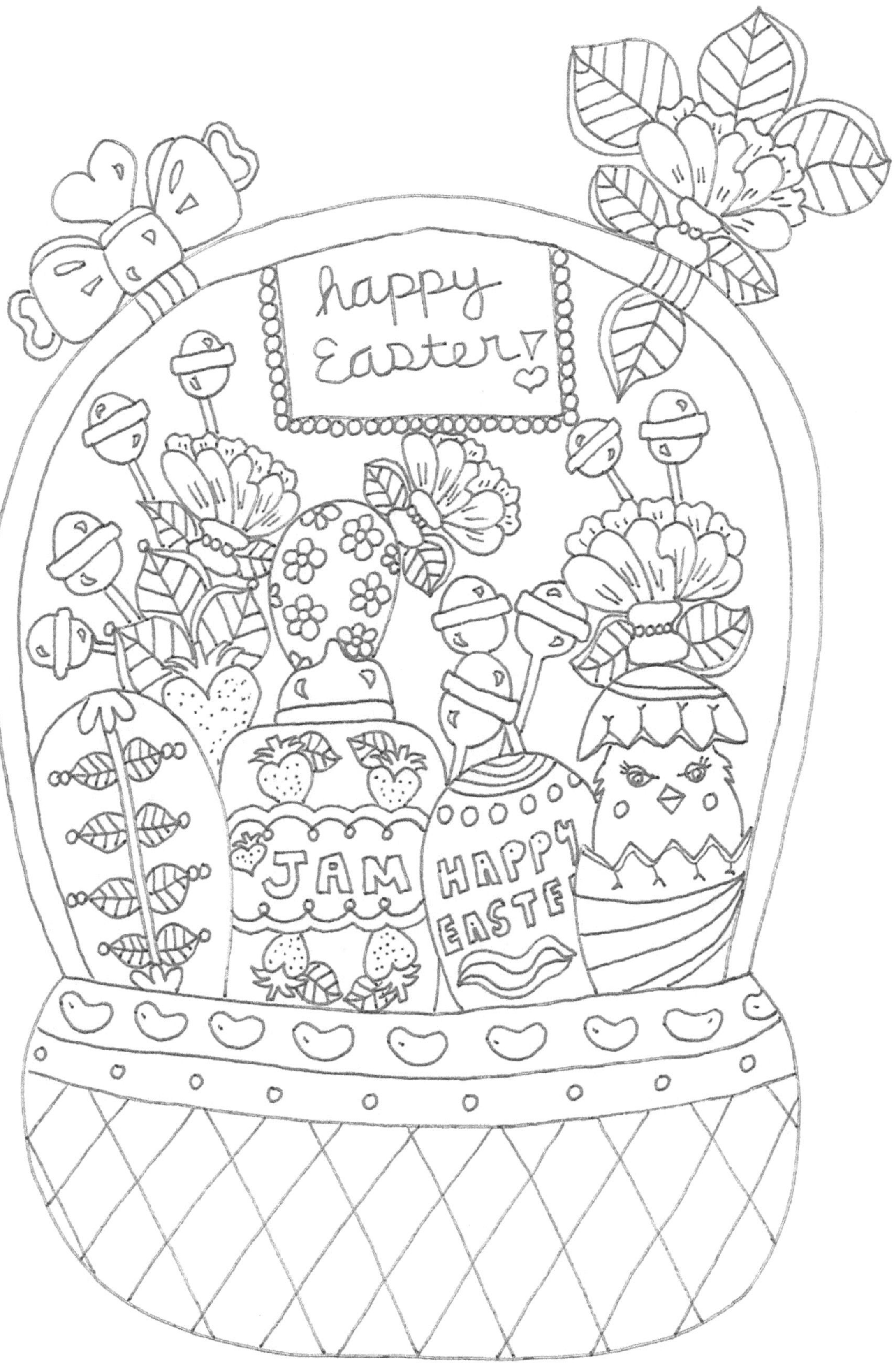

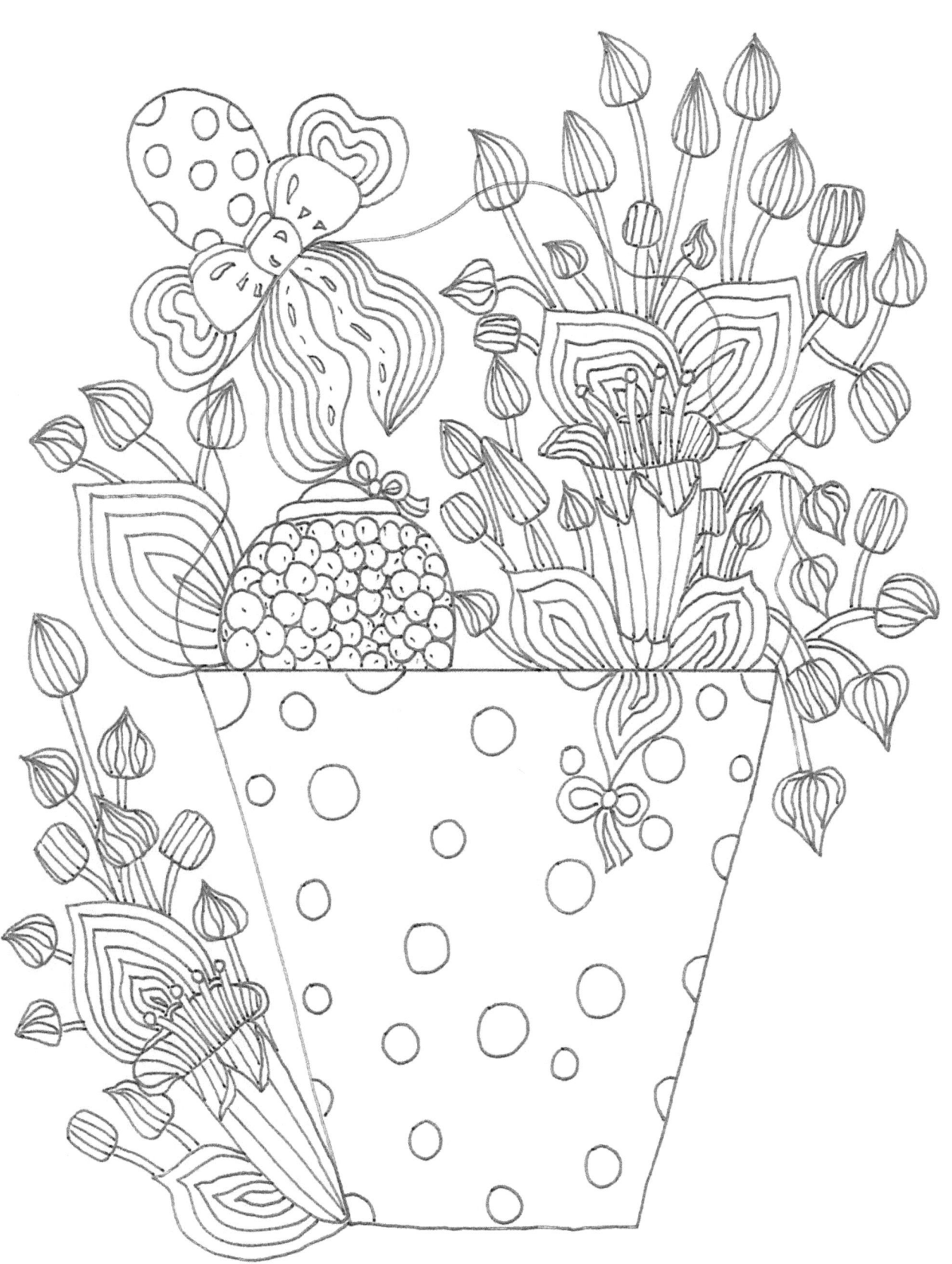

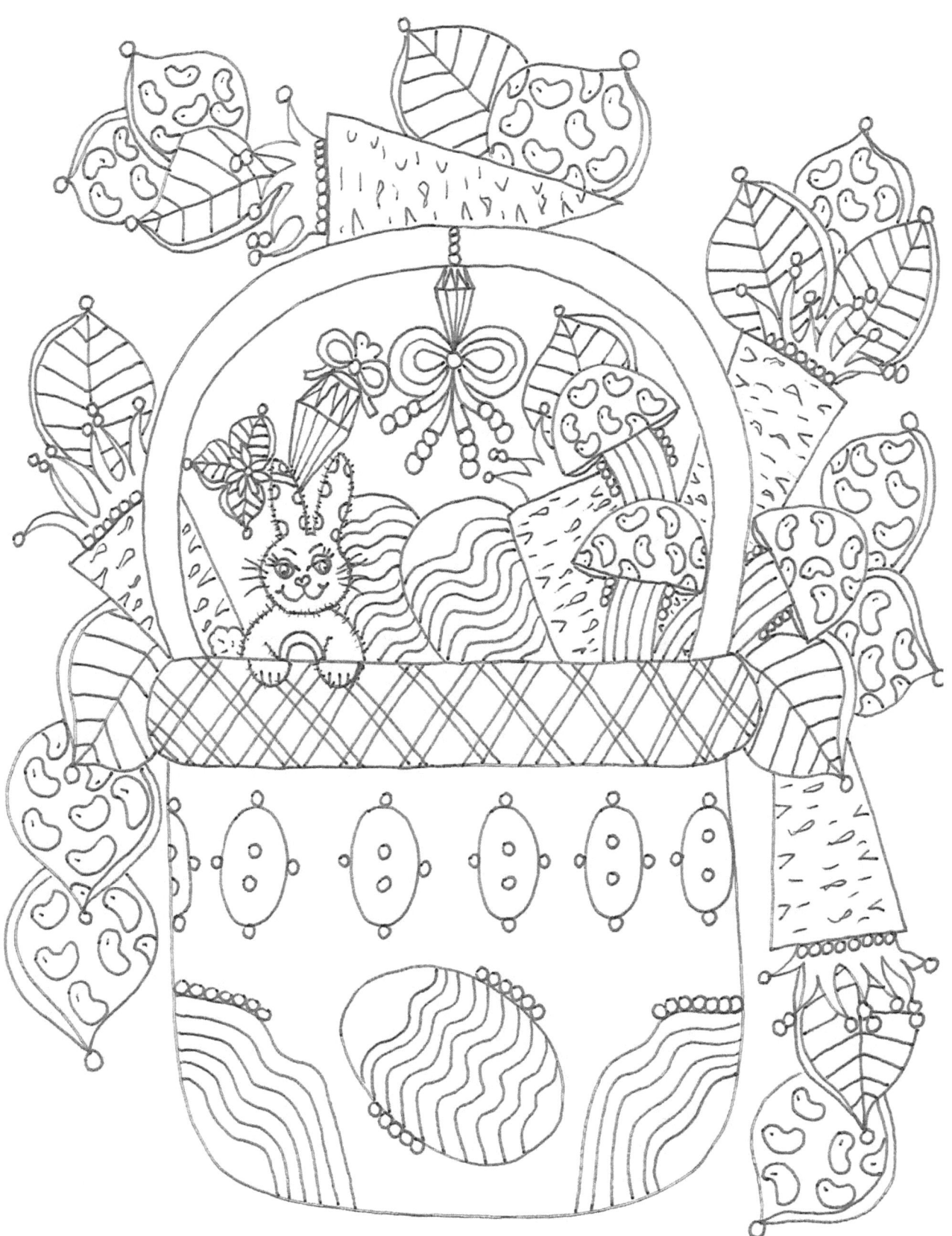

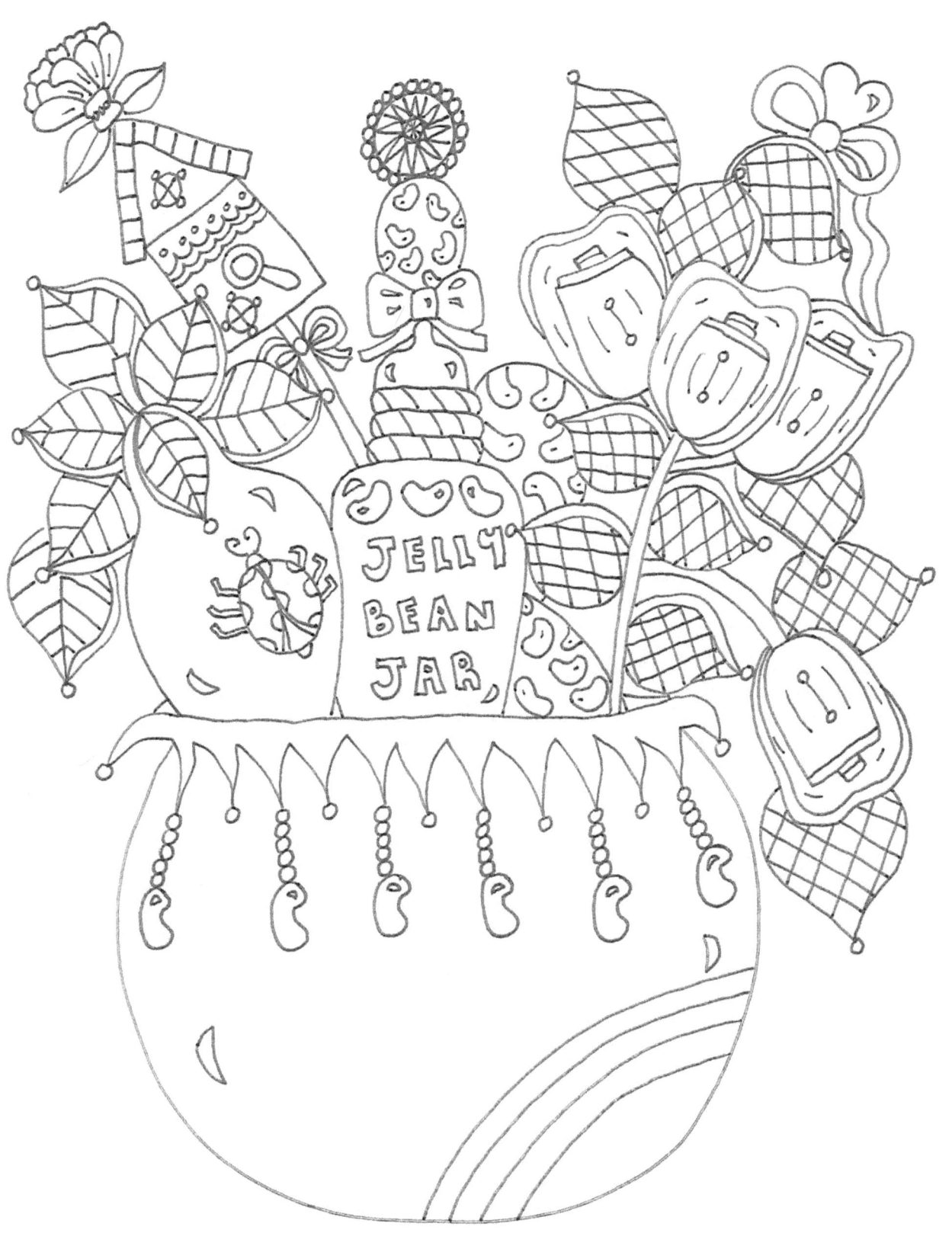

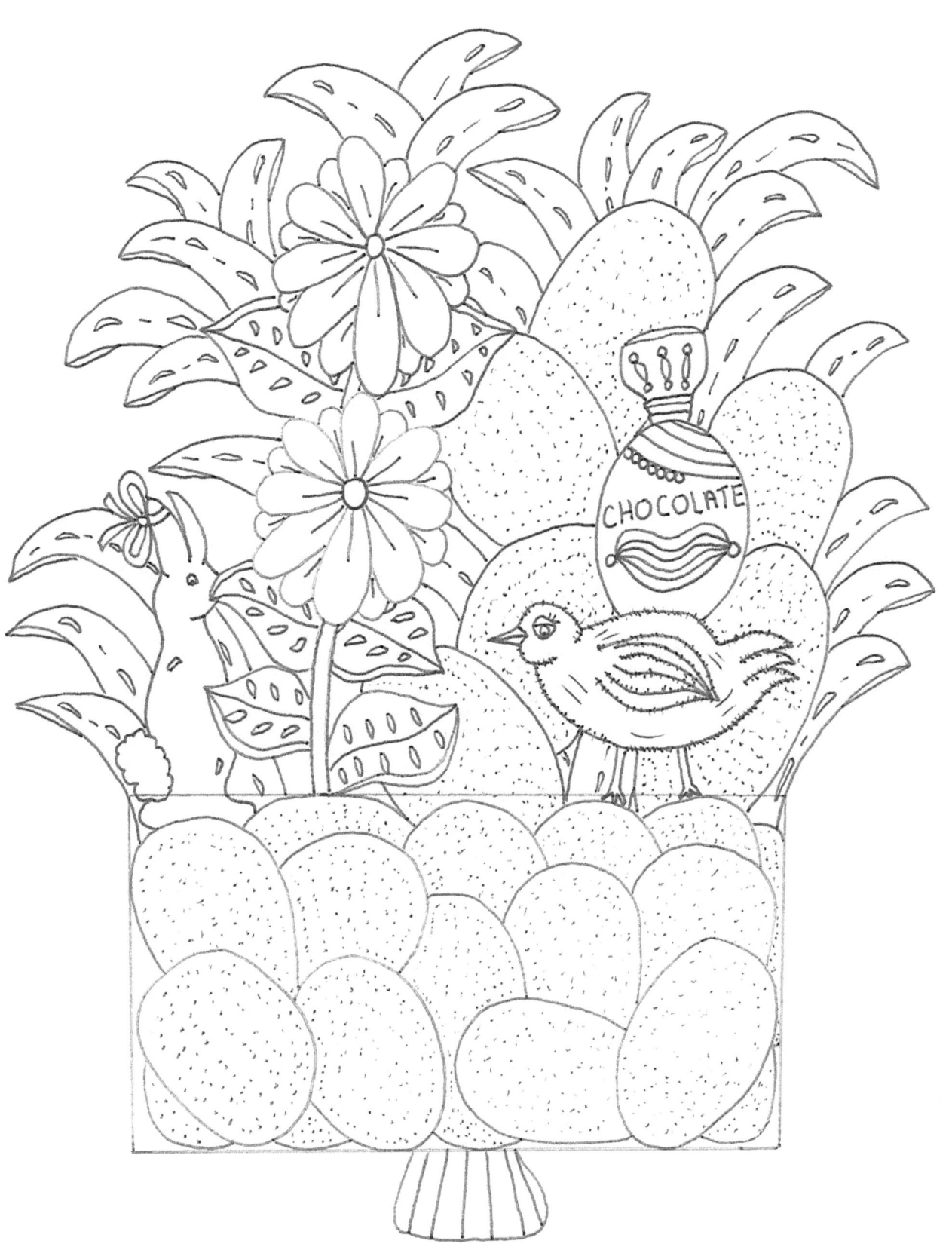

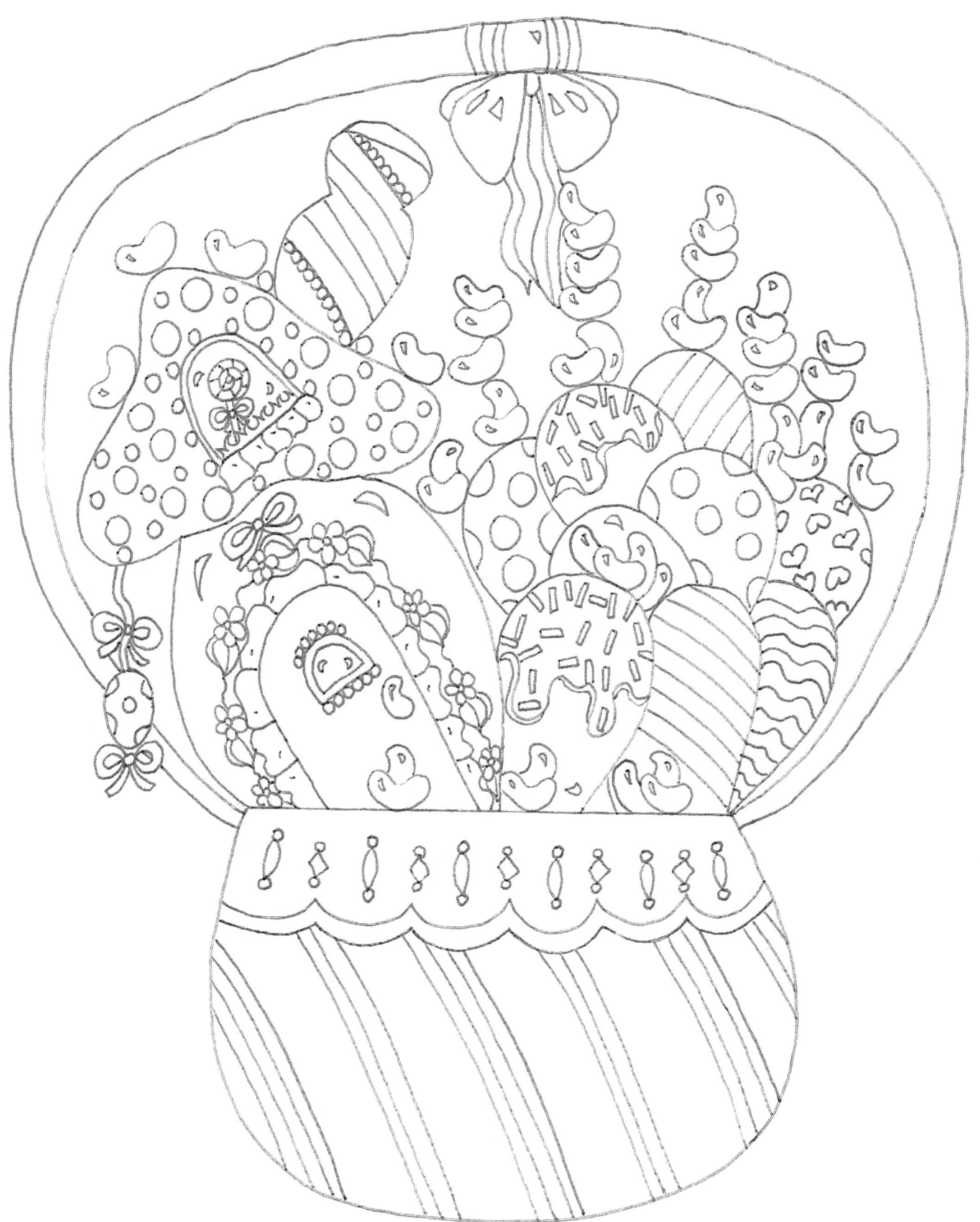

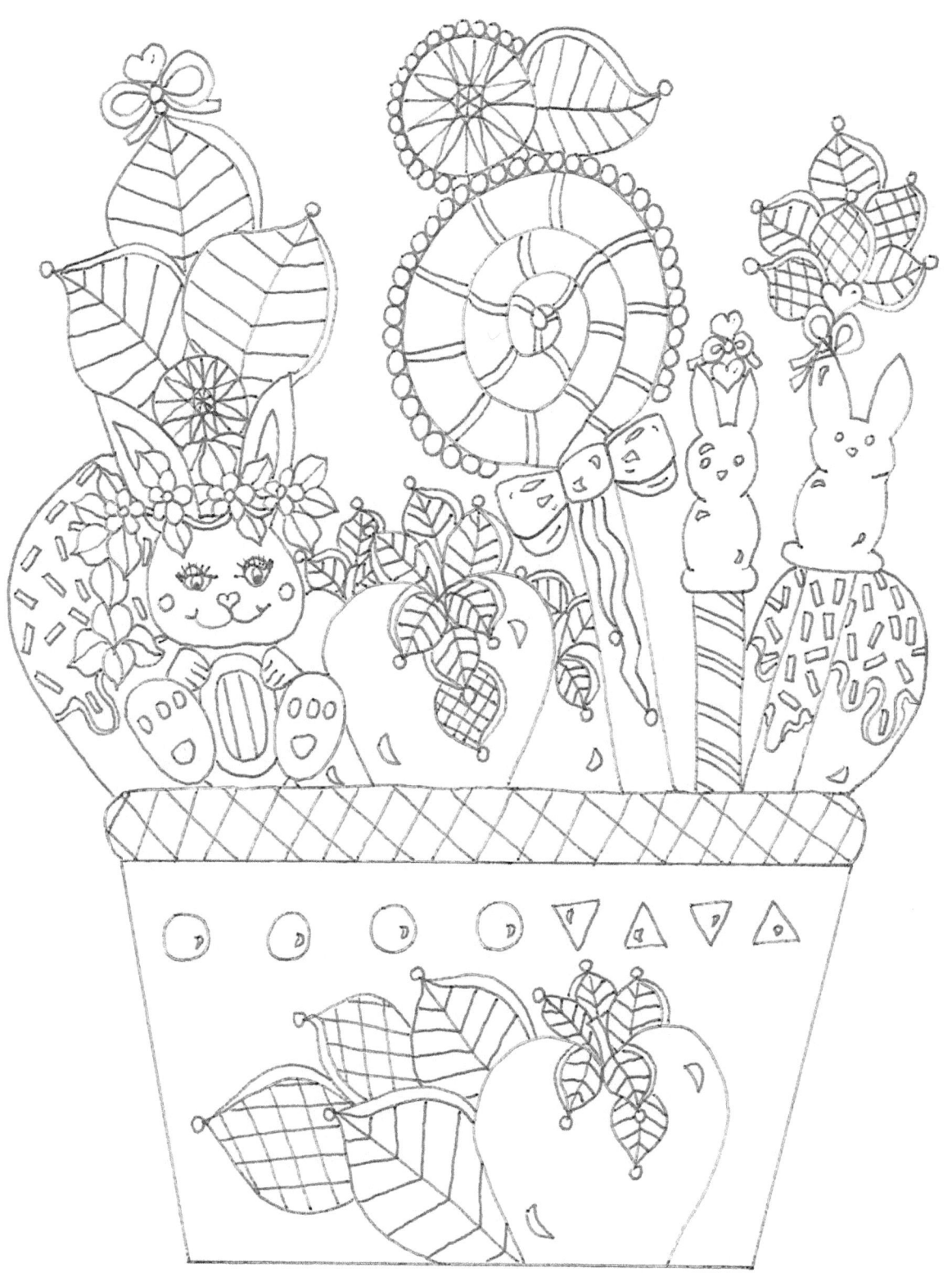

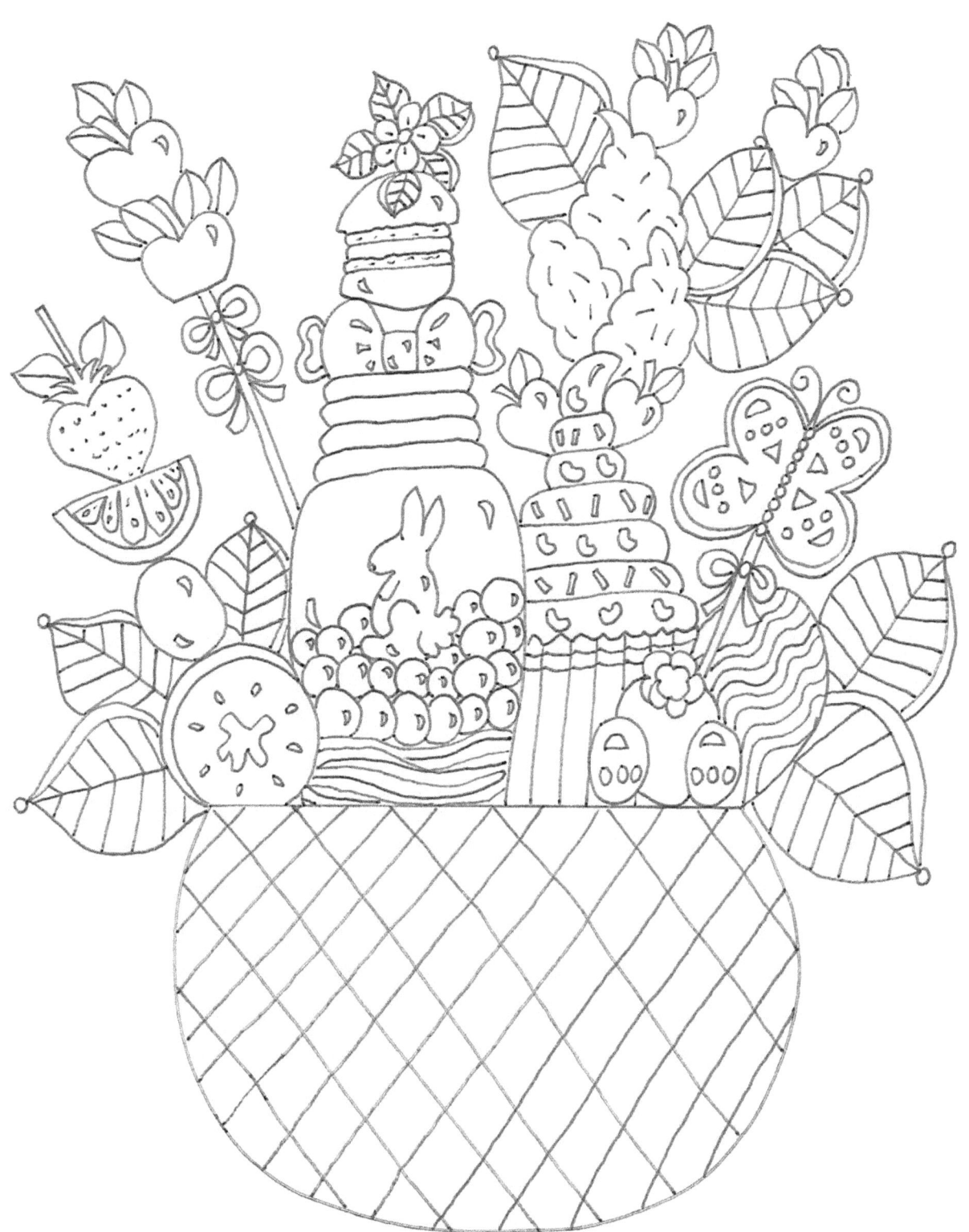

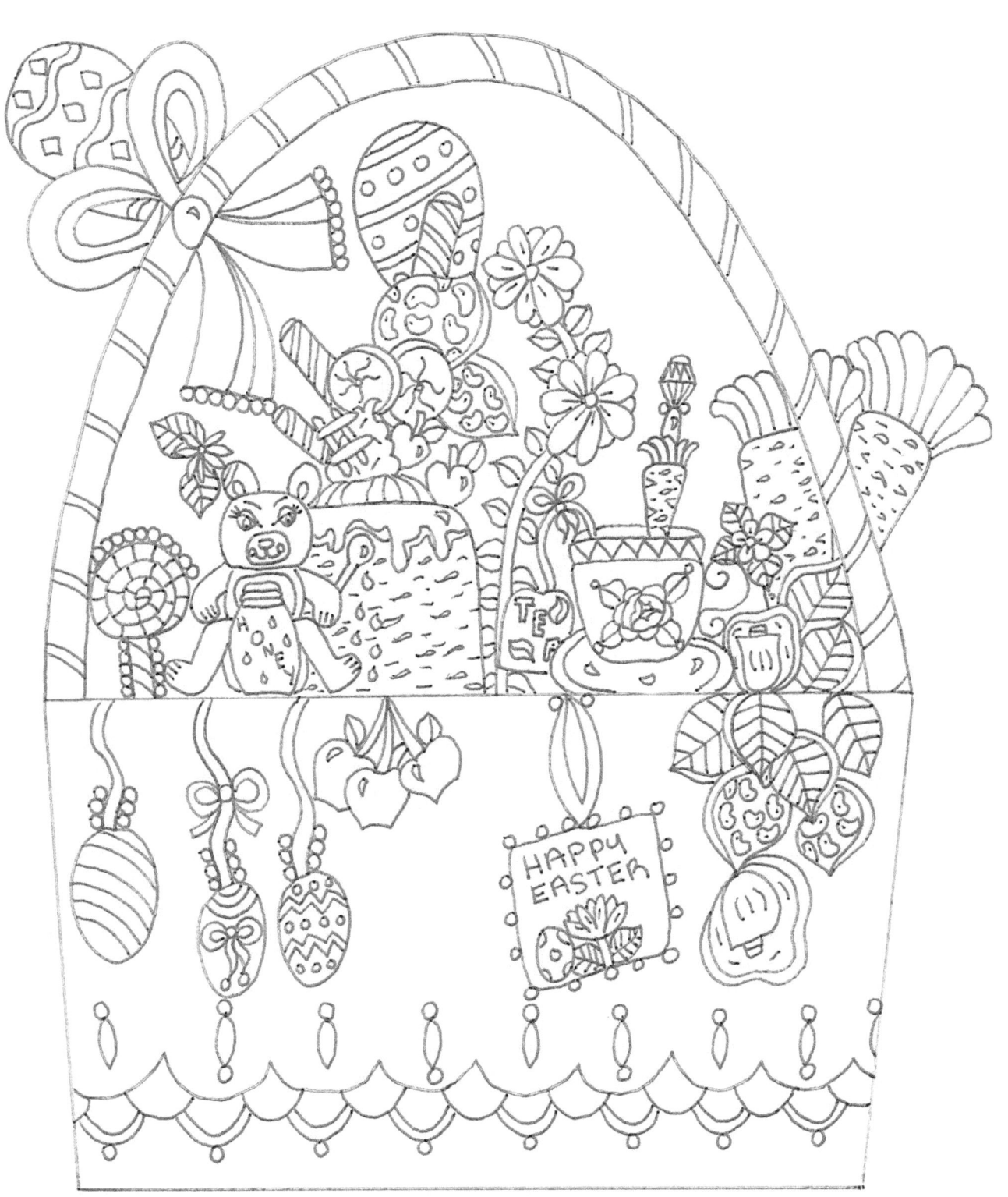

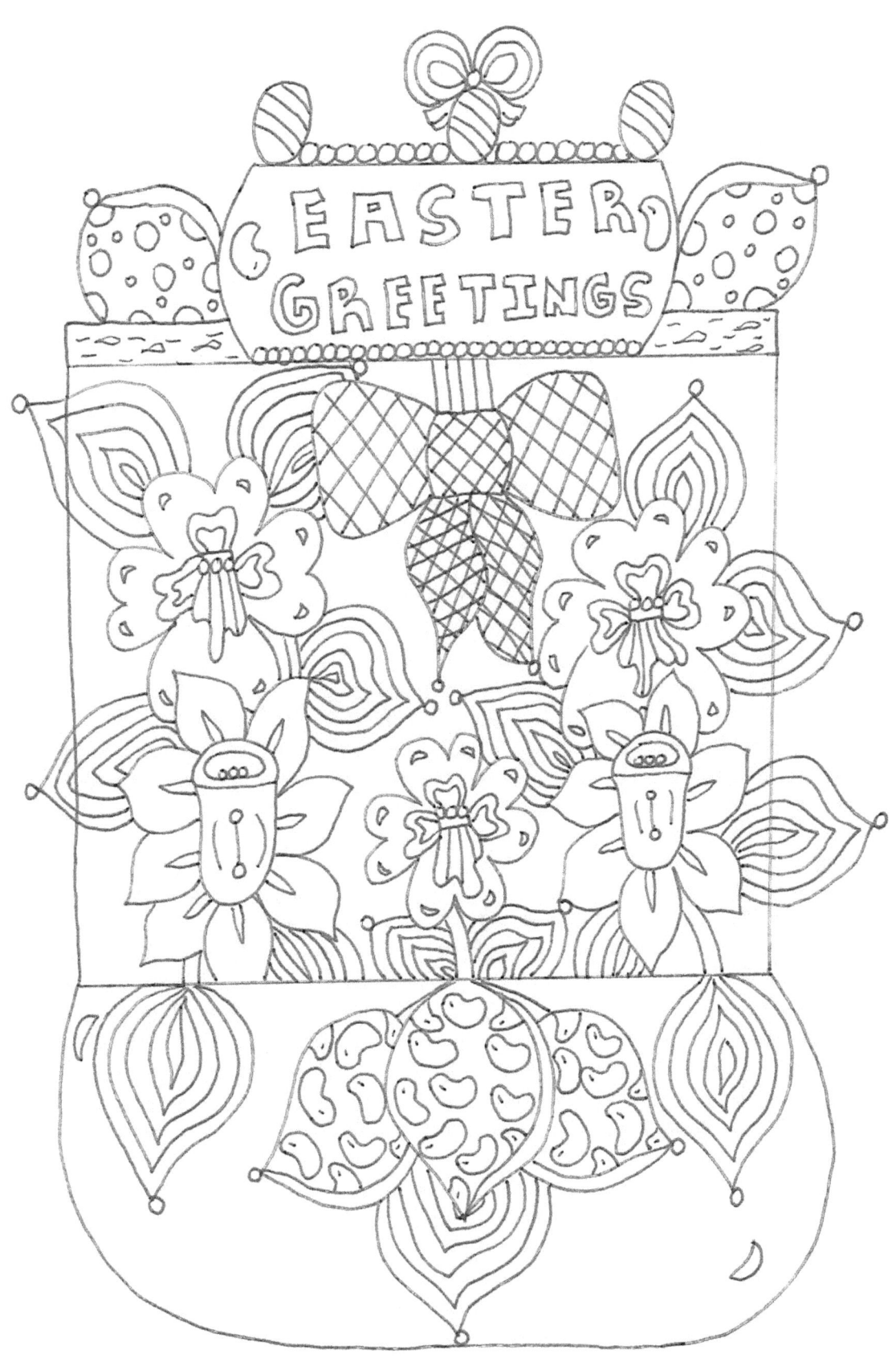

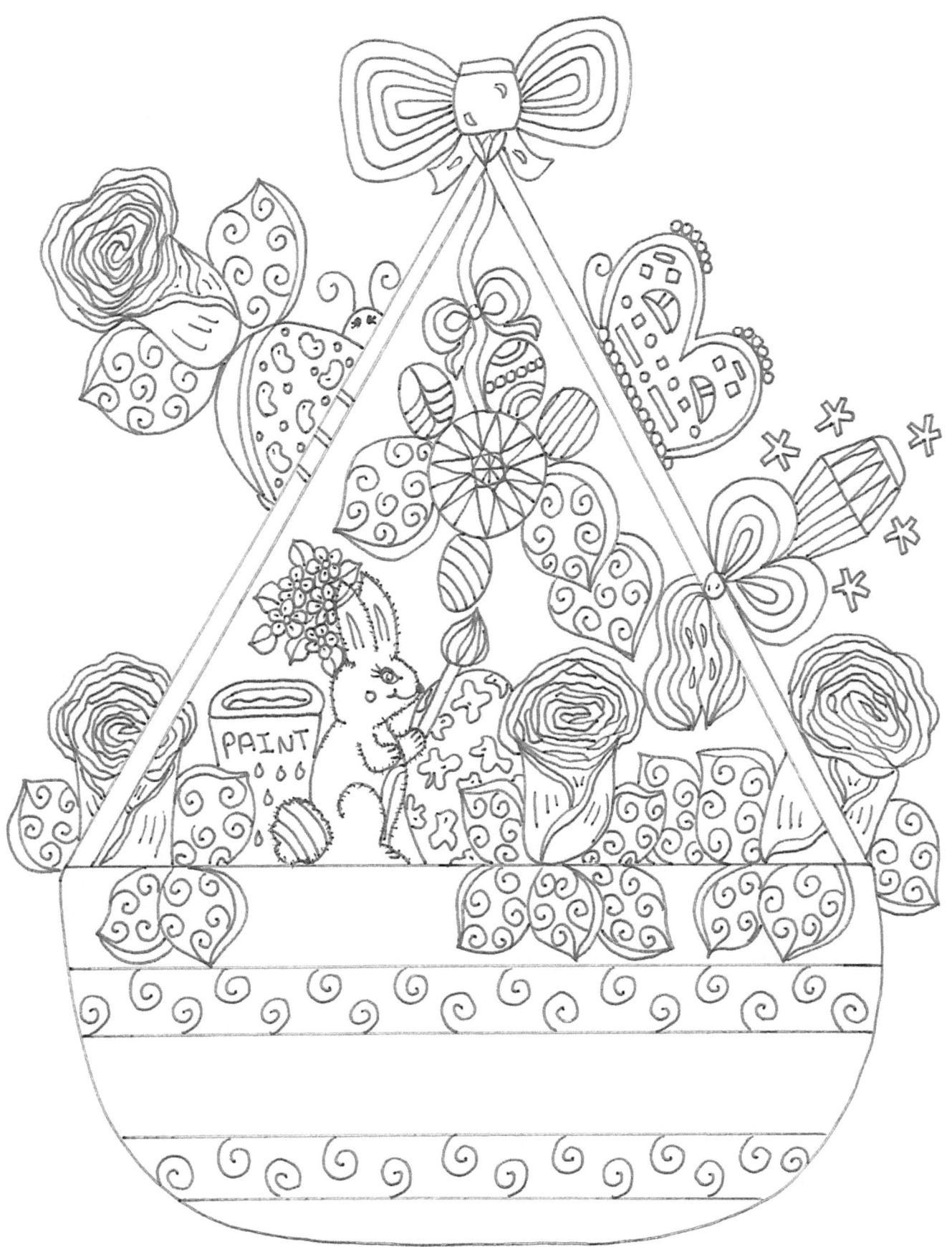

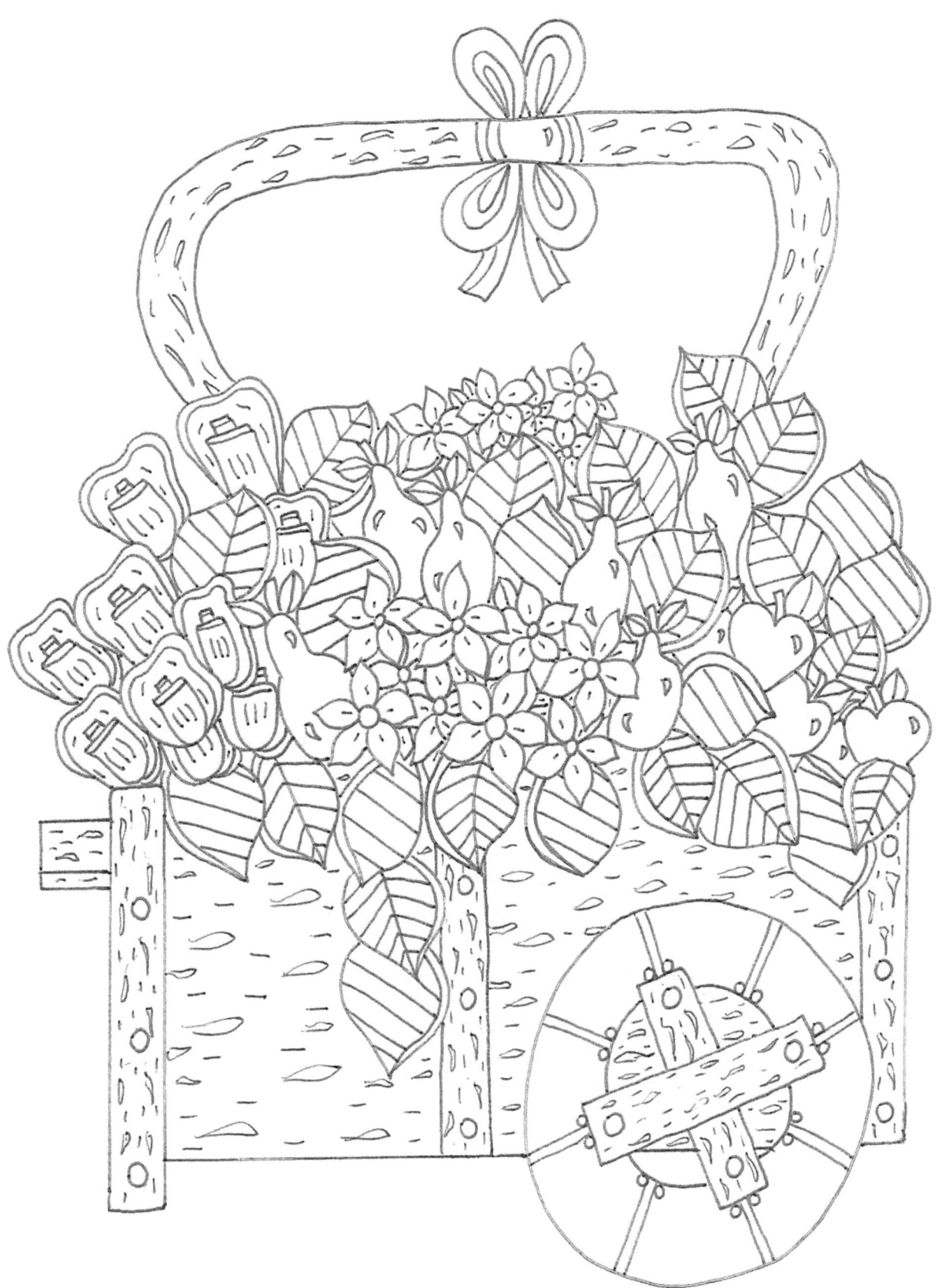

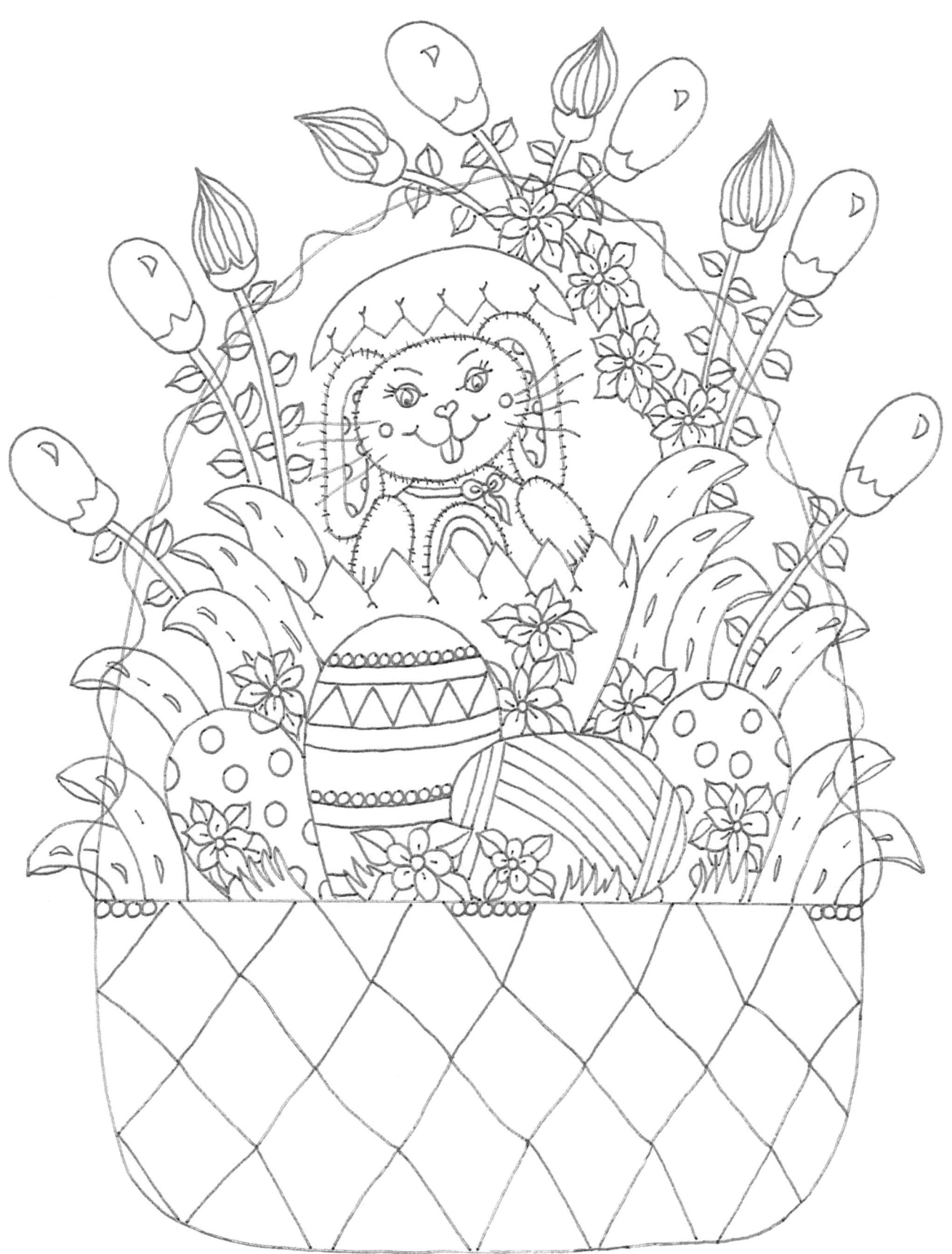

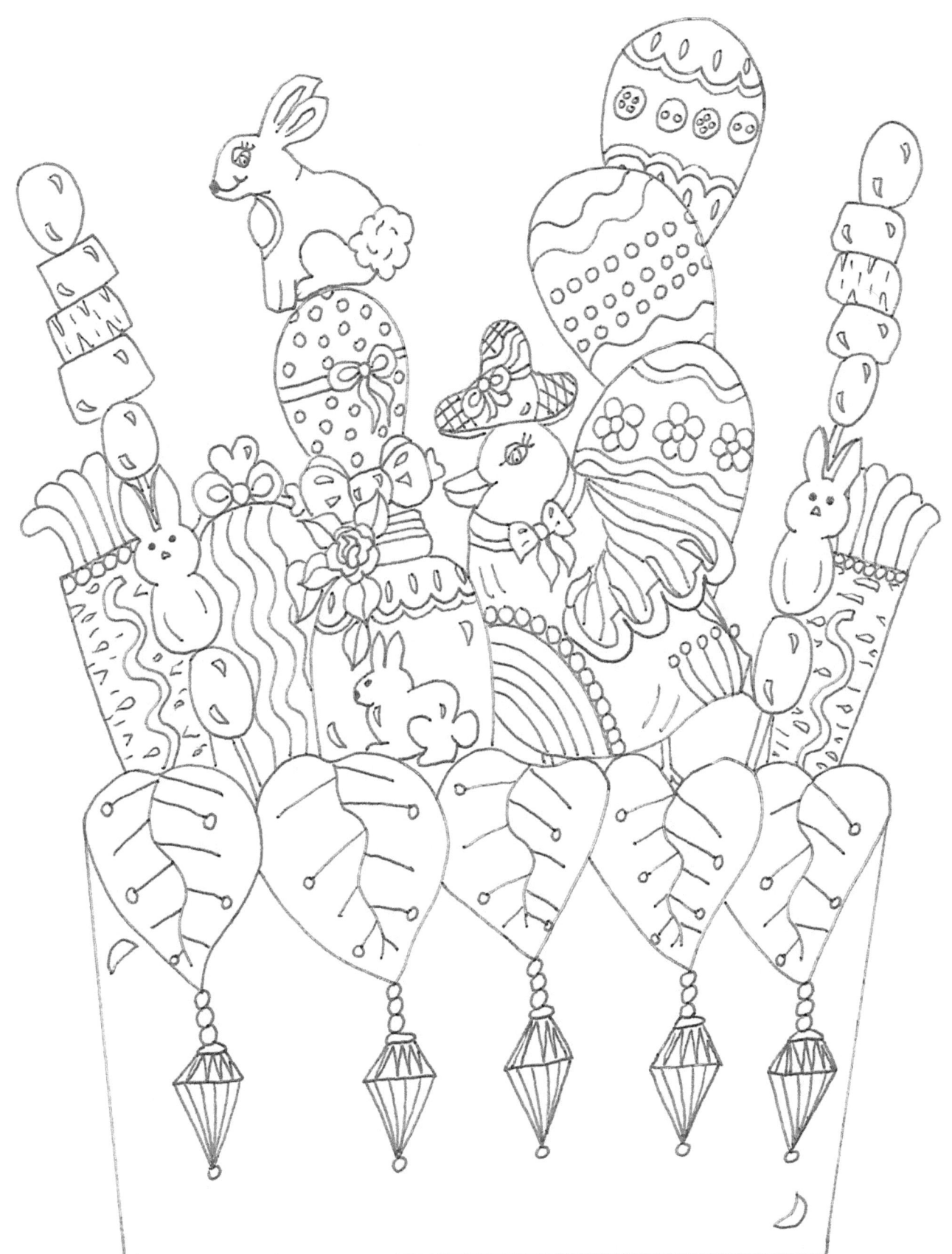

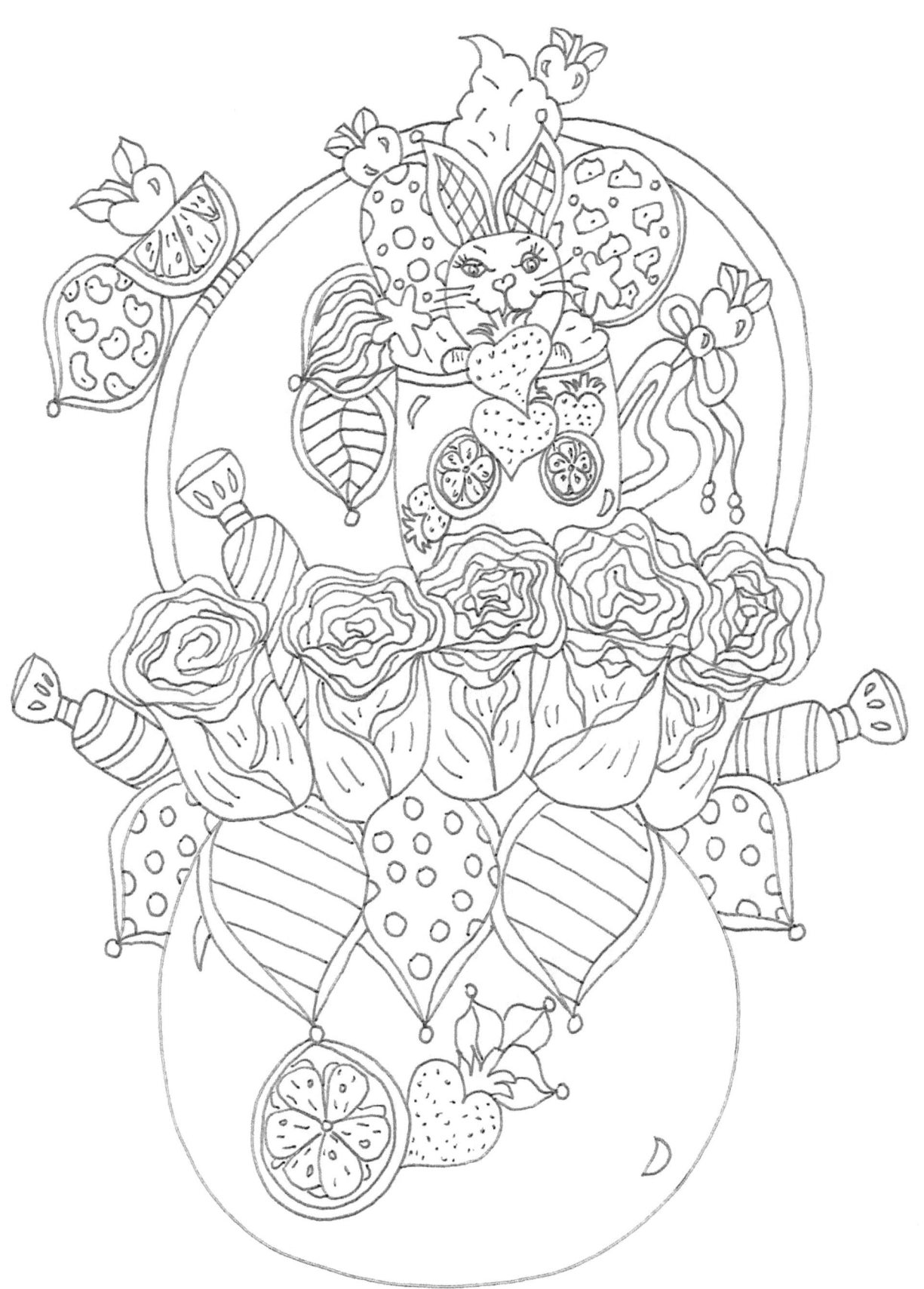

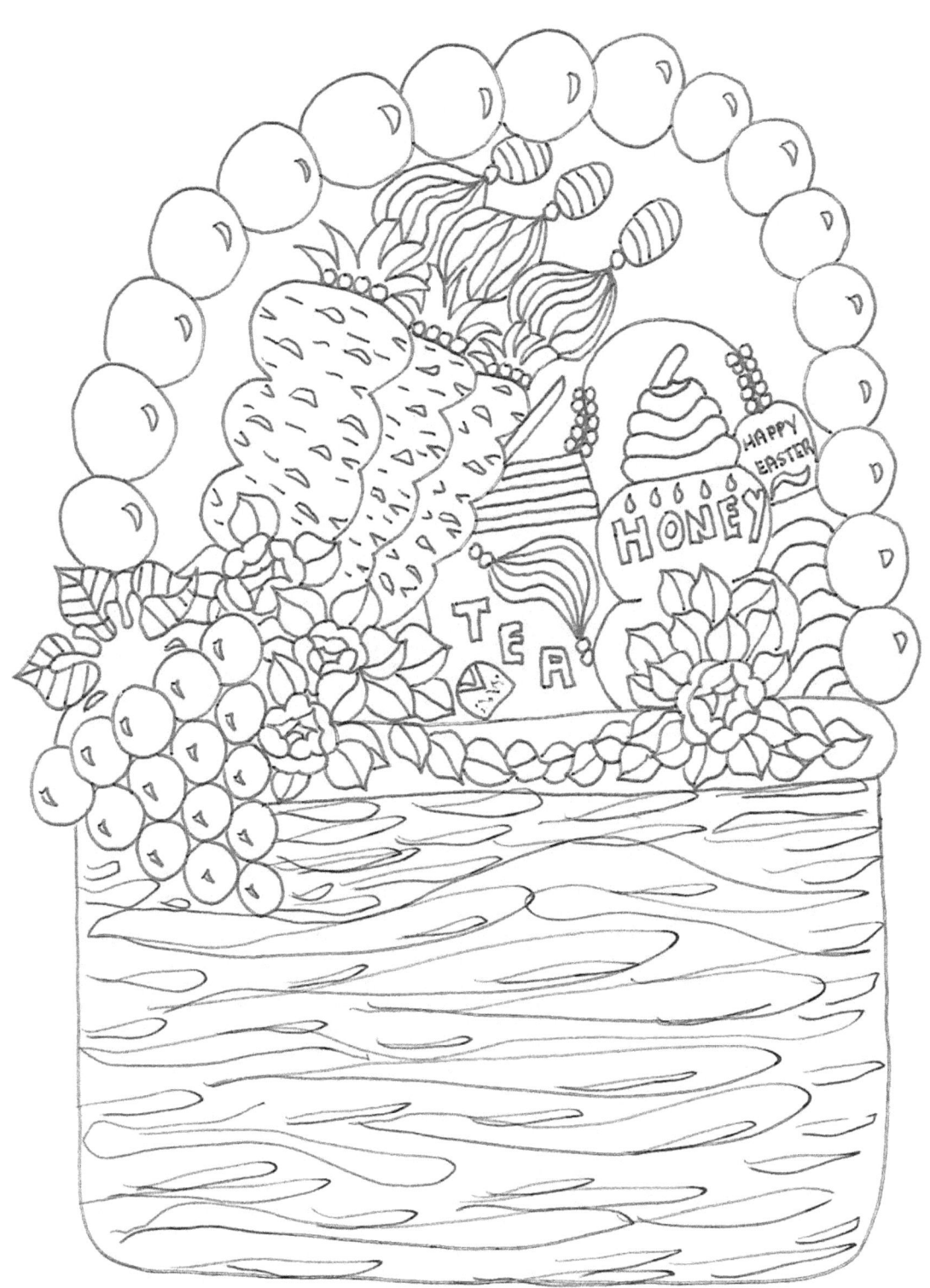

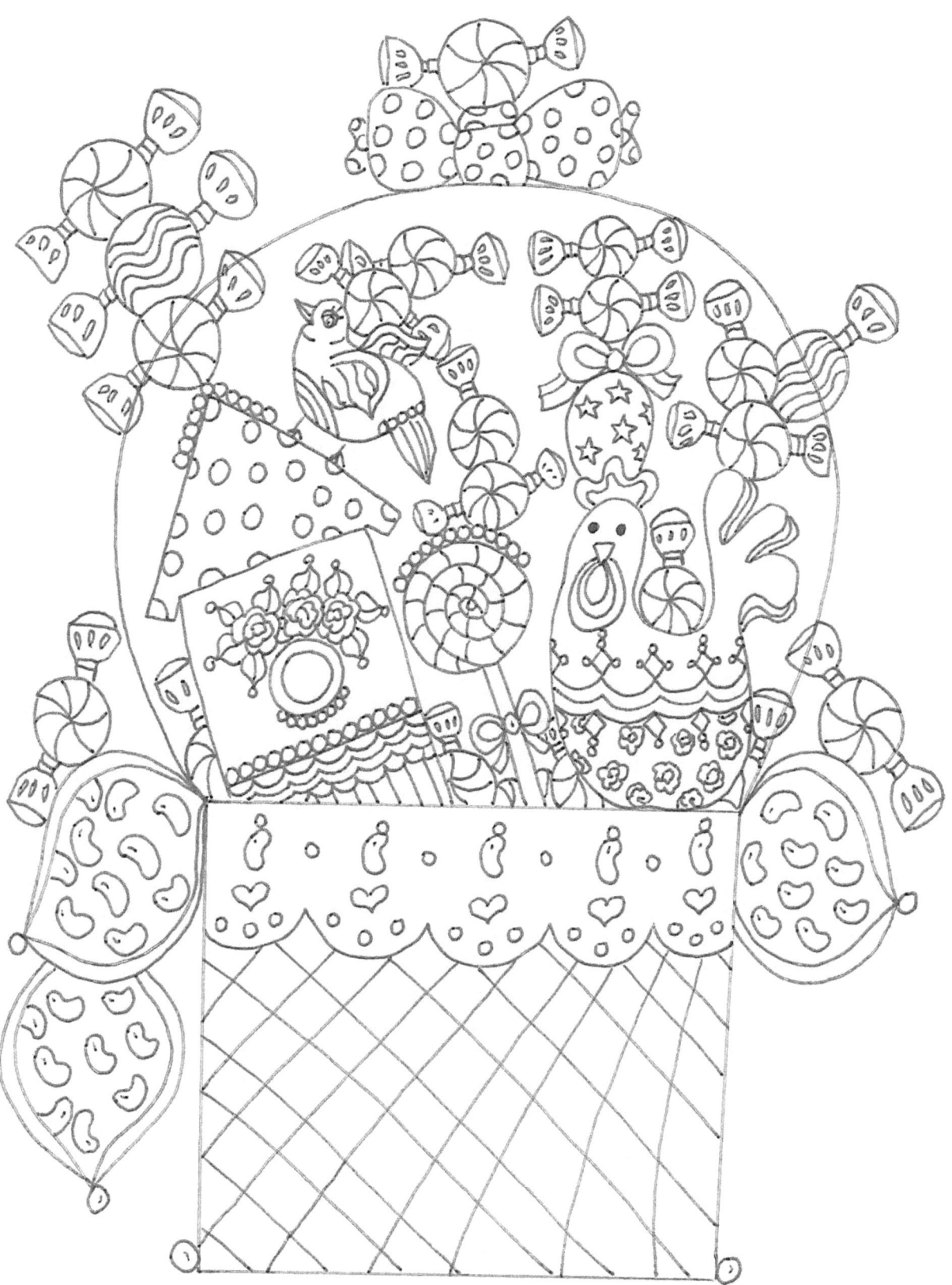

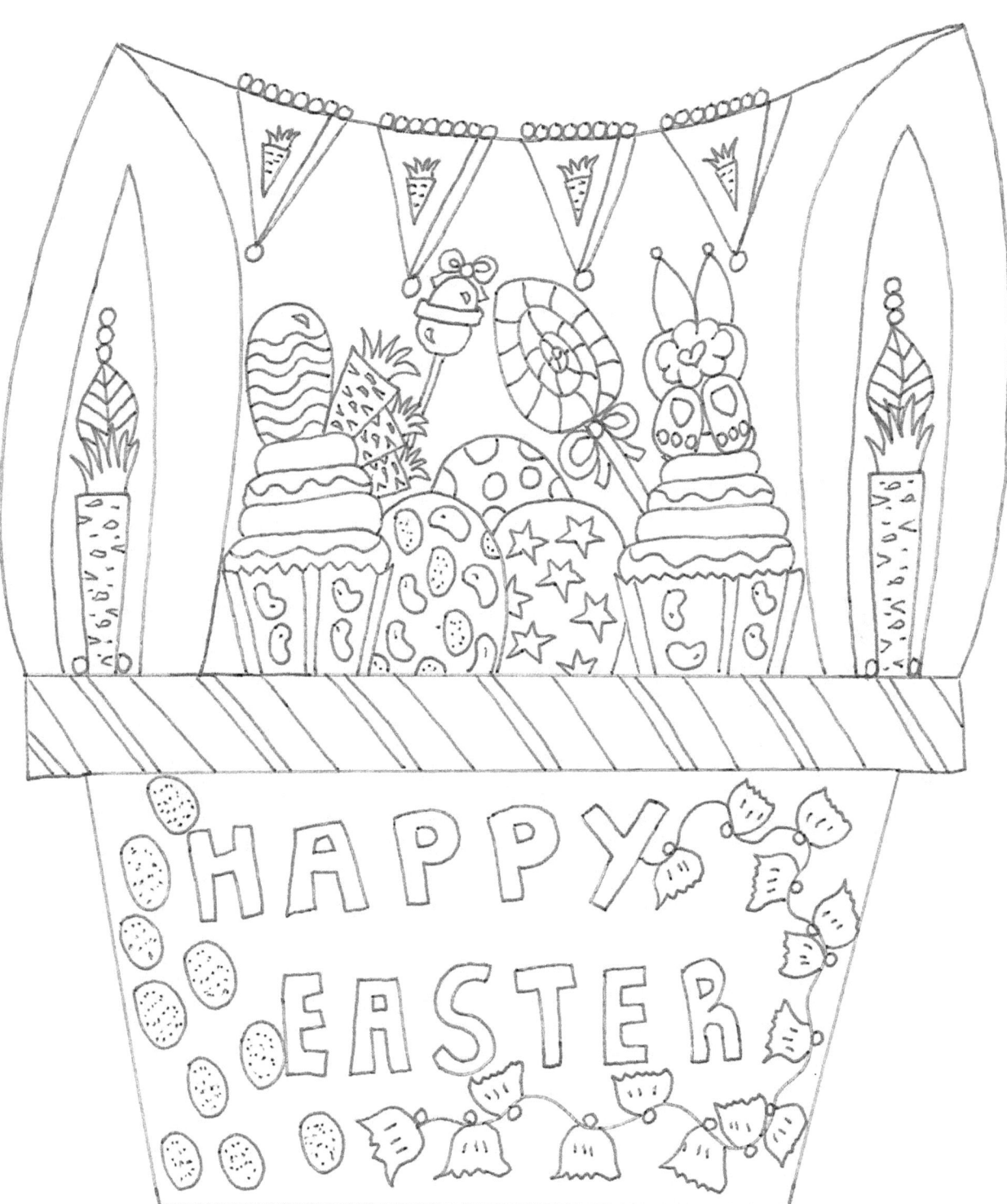

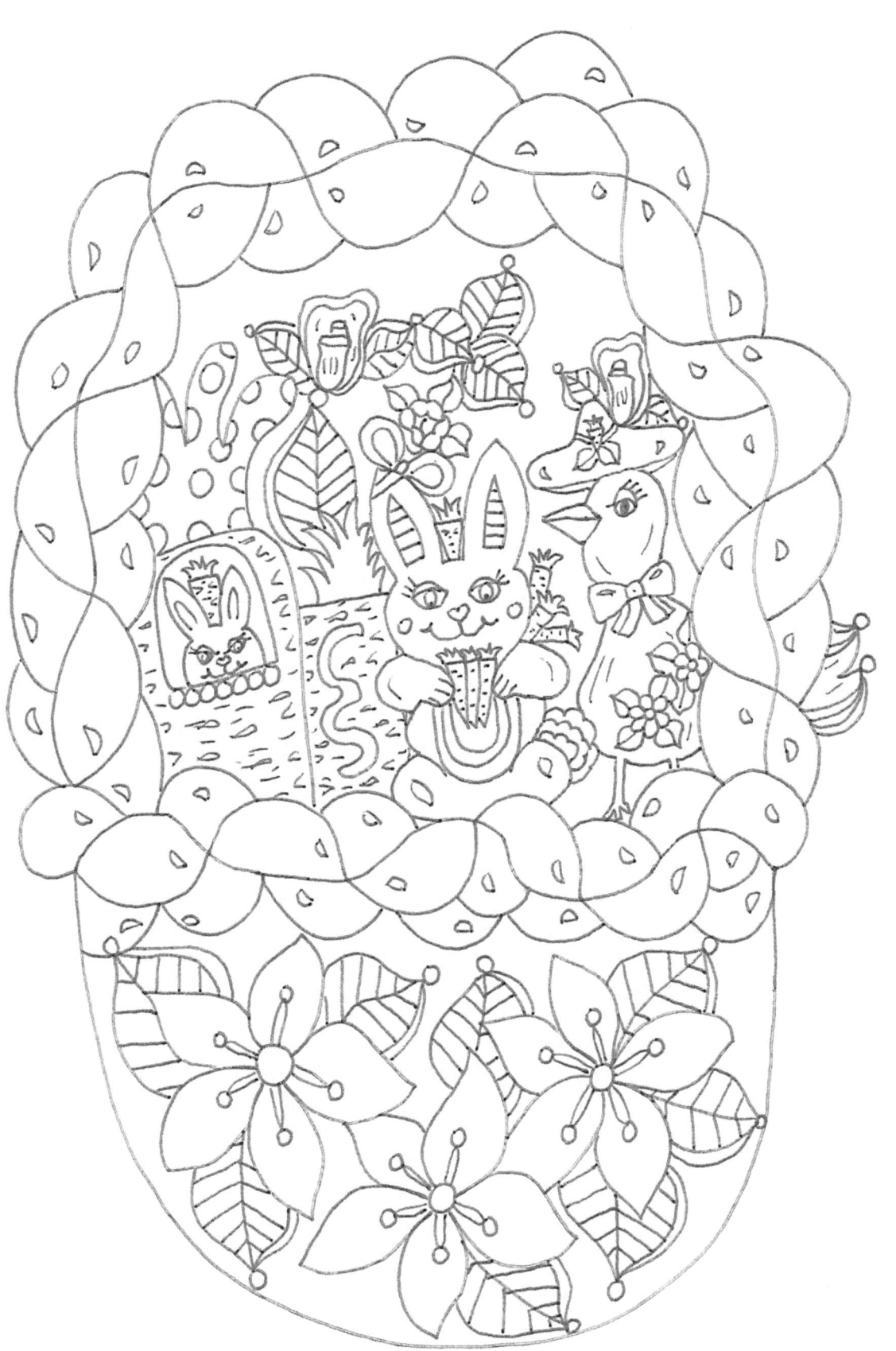

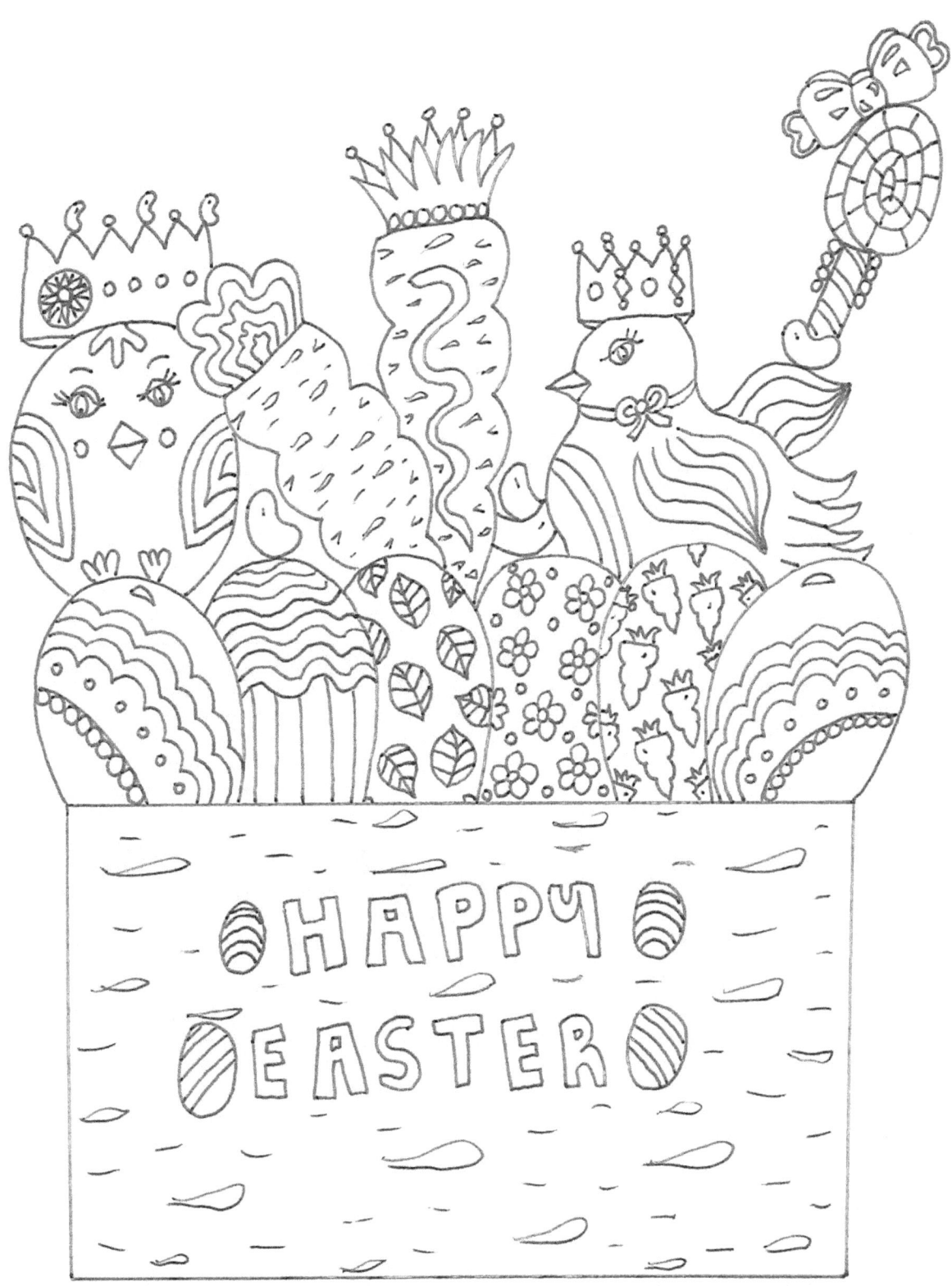

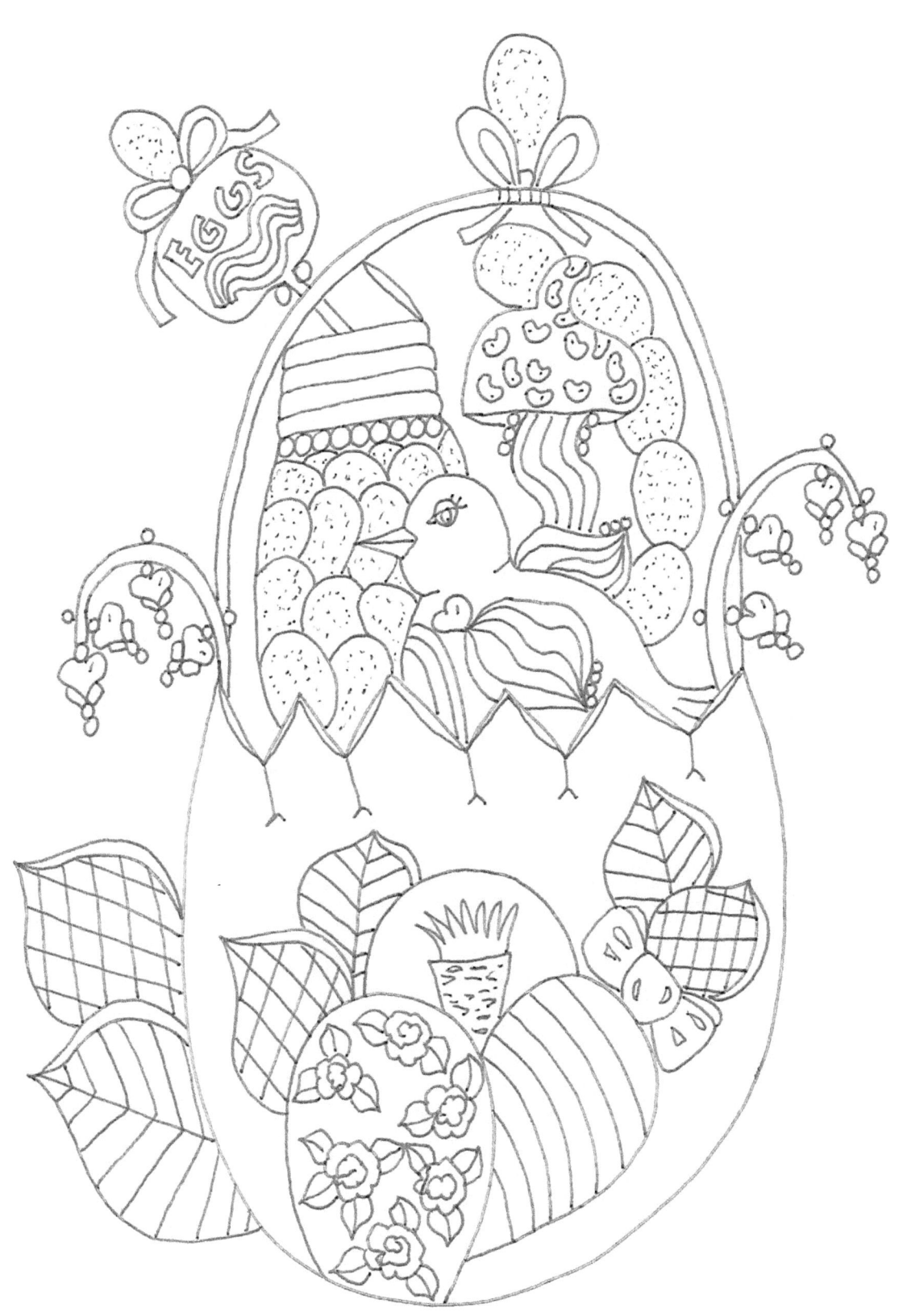

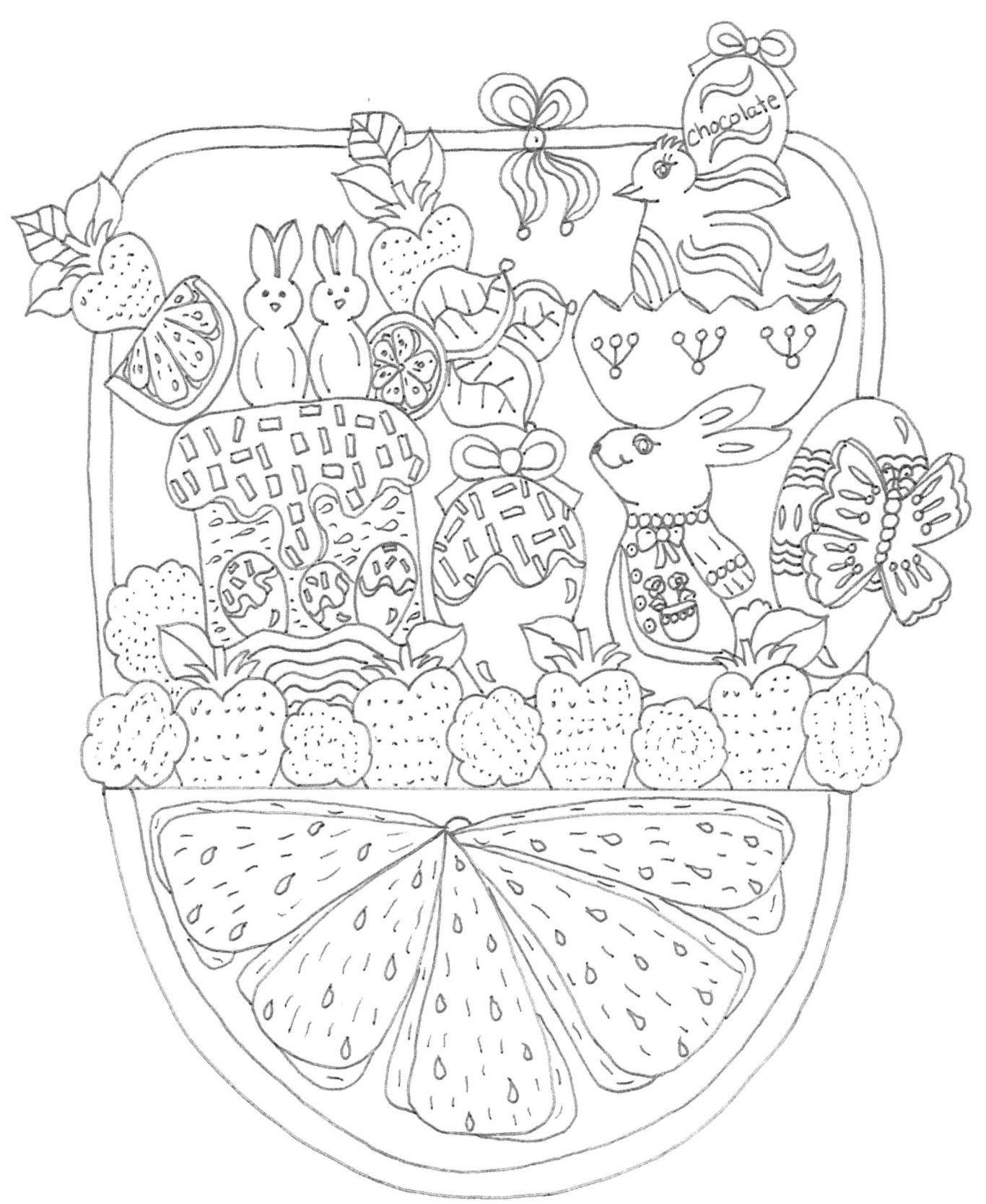

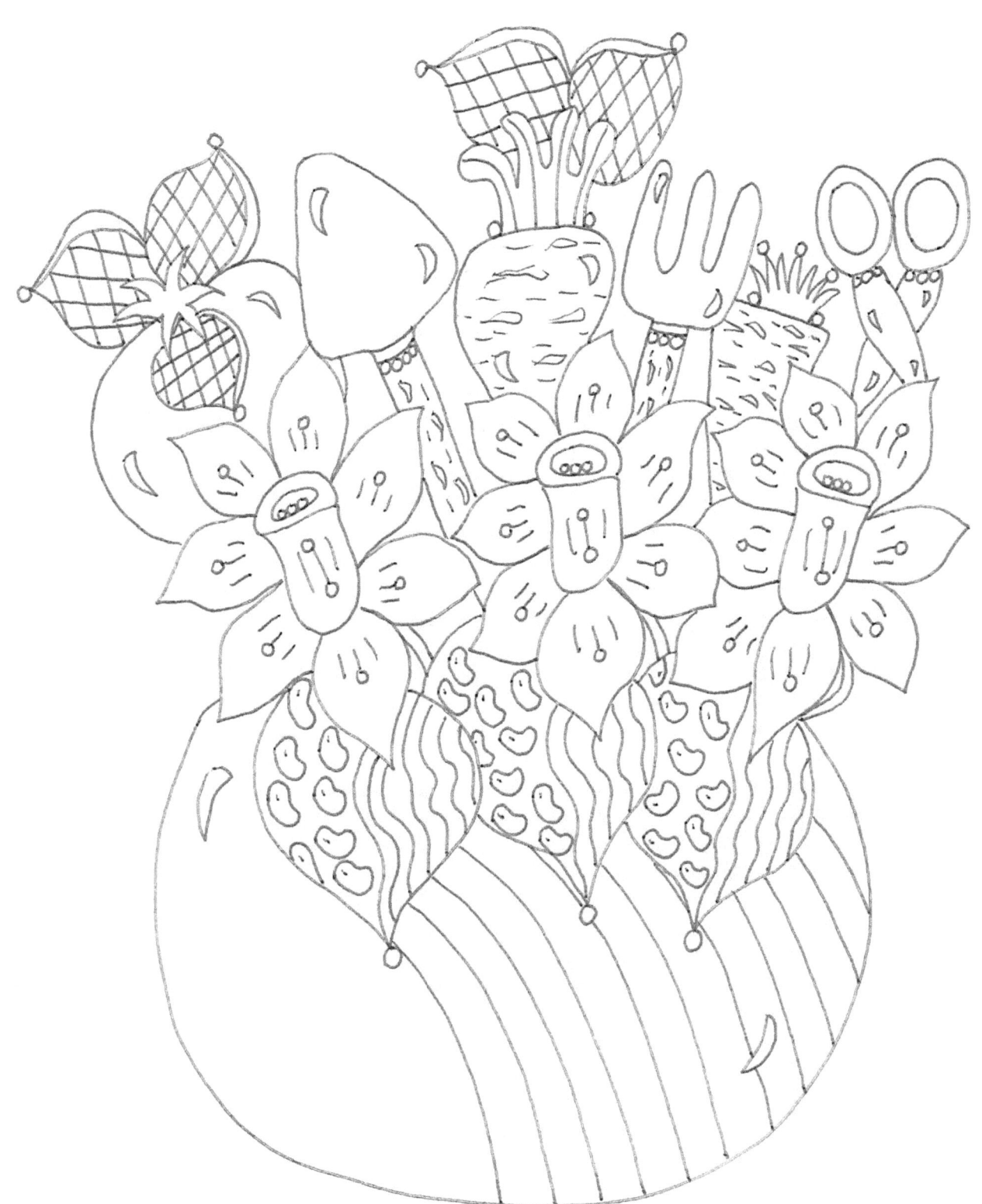

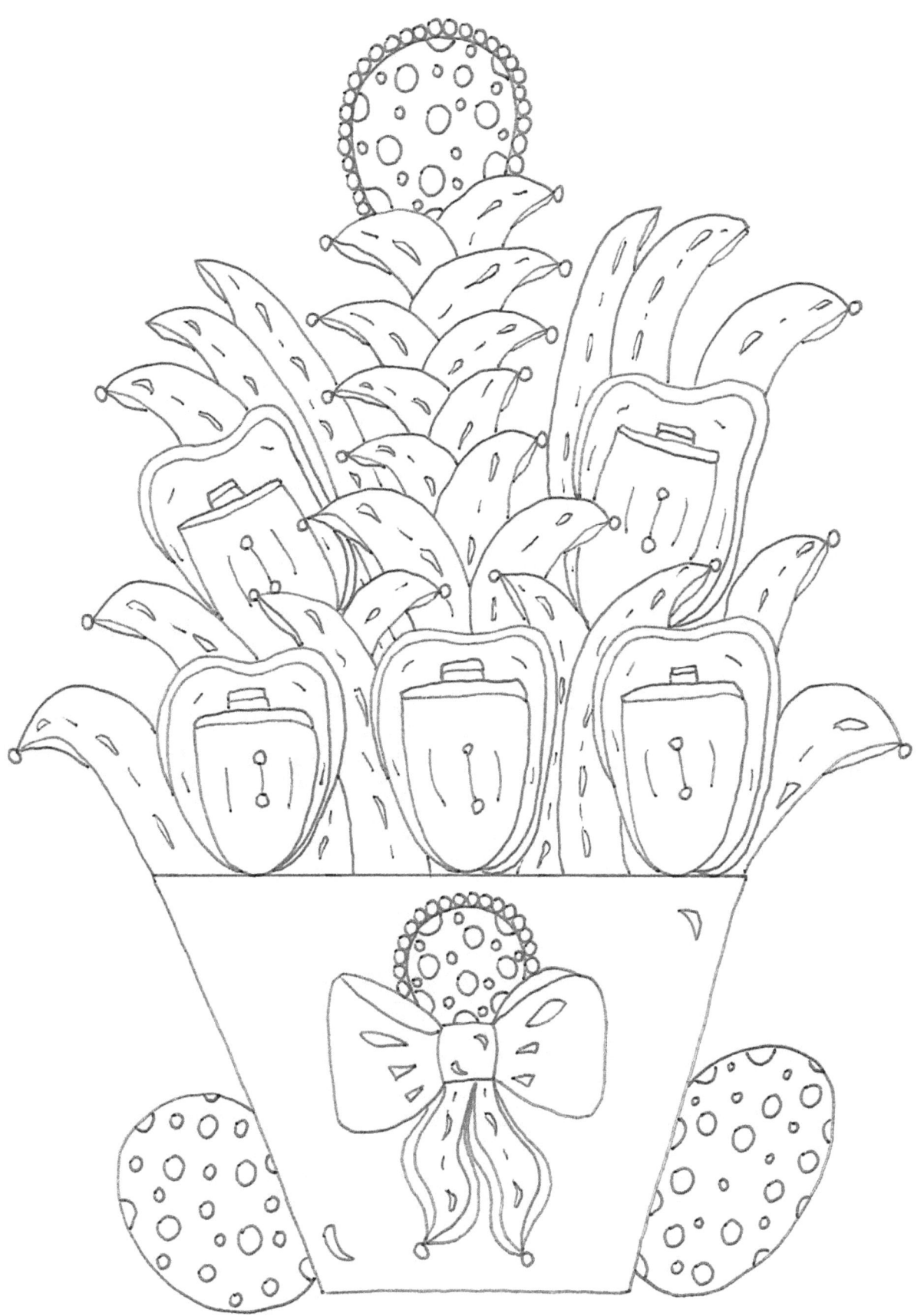

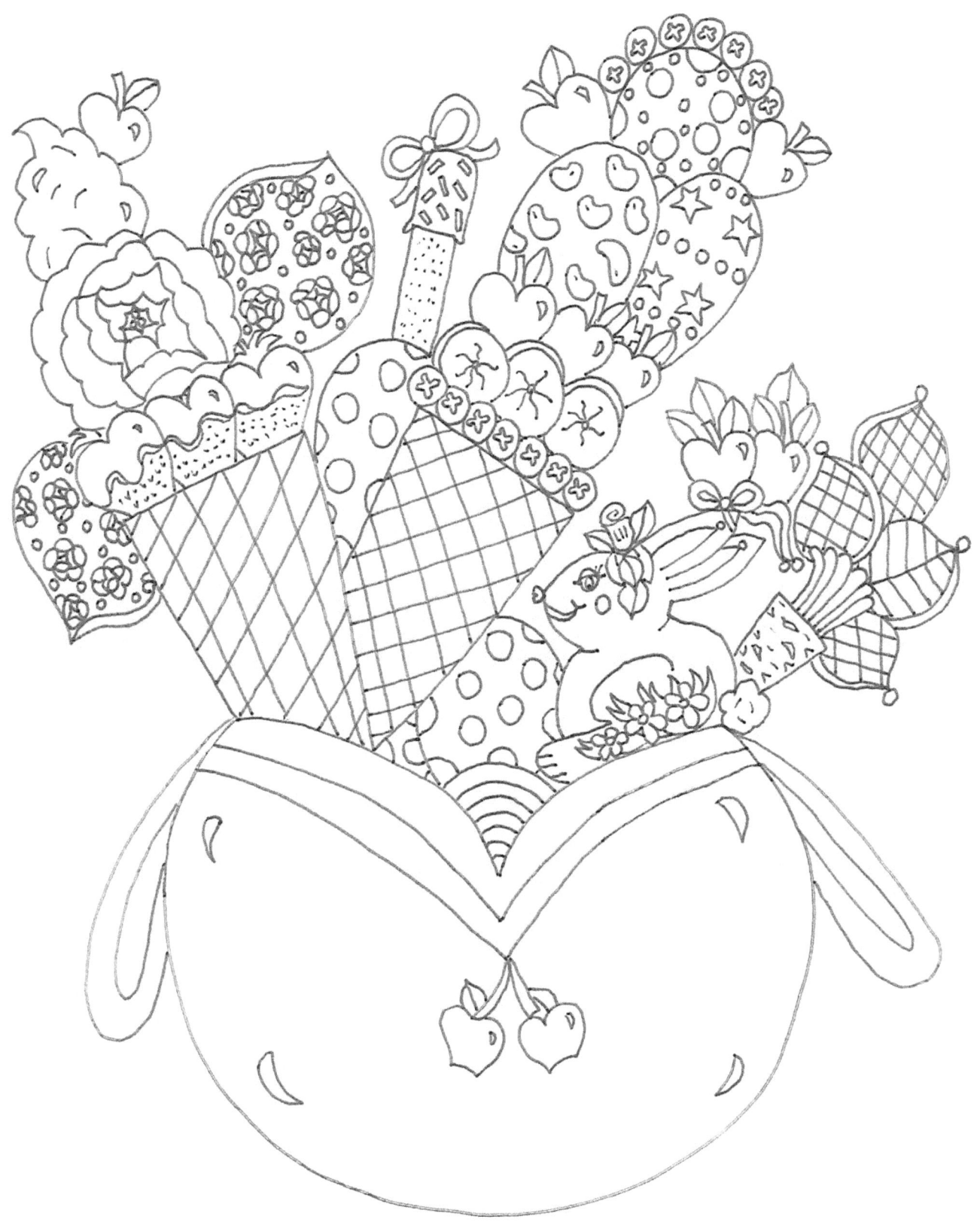

THANK YOU FOR PURCHASING EASTER BASKETS ADULT COLORING BOOK. YOU CAN CHECK OUT MY OTHER COLORING BOOKS LISTED BELOW WHICH CAN BE PURCHASED AT AMAZON.COM:

- VINTAGE PARIS BAKE SHOP (Adult)
- VINTAGE WINE GARDEN (Adult)
- ICE CREAM MADNESS (Adult)
- ICE CREAM MADNESS VOLUME 2 (Adult)
- TEA & COFFEE TROPICAL TREASURES (Adult)
- TEA & COFFEE OCEAN TREASURES (Adult)
- TEA & COFFEE TREASURES (Adult)
- BOTANICAL FLOWERS & MANDALAS (Adult)
- MAJESTIC FALL (Adult)
- A VERY RETRO CHRISTMAS (Adult)
- MAGICAL DESSERTS (Kids)
- MAGICAL DESSERTS VOLUME 2 (Kids)
- MAGICAL DESSERTS VOLUME 3 (Kids)
- FASHION DOLLS (Adult)
- FAIRIES IN THE FLOWER GARDEN (Adult)
- MERMAID'S WONDERLAND SEA OF ENCHANTMENT (Adult)
- CHRISTMAS DESSERTS
- VALENTINE'S DAYDREAMS COLORING BOOK (Adult)
- VALENTINE'S DAY DELIGHTS (Adult)
- VALENTINE'S FLOWERS & DESSERTS (Adult)
- VALENTINE'S DAY DESSERTS (Adult)
- VALENTINE'S DAY ANIMALS & Sweets (Kids)
- VALENTINE DAY'S FLOWERS (Adult)
- A VERY RUSTIC VALENTINE'S DAY (Adult)
- ELEGANT FLOWERS (Adult)
- ST. PATRICK'S DAY BLESSINGS (Adult)
- A HAPPY ST. PATTY'S DAY (Kids)
- ST. PATRICK'S DAY DESSERTS (Adult)
- ST. PATRICK DAY FLOWERS (Adult)
- SPRINGTIME FAIRIES (Adult)
- SPECTACULAR DESSERTS (Adult)
- BEAUTIFUL SPRINGTIME FLOWERS (Adult)
- MERMAID DESSERTS (Adult)
- FLORAL DELIGHTS (Adult)
- FABULOUS SPRINGTIME WREATHS (Adult)
- DELICIOUS SPRINGTIME DESSERTS (Adult)
- CHARMING EASTER FLOWERS (Adult)
- EASTER WONDERLAND (Adult)
- EASTER BLESSINGS (Adult)
- LOVELY EASTER WREATHS (Adult)

IF YOU ENJOYED YOUR COLORING EXPERIENCE, PLEASE TELL OTHERS ABOUT IT BY WRITING A REVIEW ON AMAZON.COM UNDER THE BOOK YOU COLORED